ECO LEGENDS ALPHABET

Words by Robin Feiner

A is for **Al** Gore.
This former U.S. Vice President helped bring climate change to the world's attention with his Oscar-winning 2006 documentary, 'An Inconvenient Truth.' Thanks to his Nobel Peace Prize winning efforts, global warming has now become a top priority for governments worldwide. What a legend!

B is for David Brower.
Famous for the catchphrase,
"Think globally, act locally,"
he founded the Friends of the
Earth organization to lobby
environmental, social and
human rights issues. His fiery
activism and passionate desire
for an 'unspoilt world' made
him an inspiration for today's
eco-warriors.

C is for Chico Mendes. This Brazilian labor leader and conservationist fought to protect the Amazon and its indigenous peoples from deforestation by greedy developers. Sadly, his anti-logging activism led to his death in 1988, but he remains a true eco-legend to this day.

Dd

D is for **D**avid Attenborough. Perhaps more than any other person, Sir David has helped us understand and appreciate the wonders of nature. Through renowned documentaries like 'Life on Earth' and 'The Blue Planet,' he iconically narrates the beauty of our world, while reminding us of how fragile it really is.

E is for Sylvia **E**arle. Interested in the natural world from a young age, this marine biologist, explorer, author, and lecturer was named by 'Time' magazine as its first Hero for the Planet in 1998! Launching Mission Blue to establish marine protected areas around the globe, Sylvia's goal is to achieve 30% protection of the ocean by 2030.

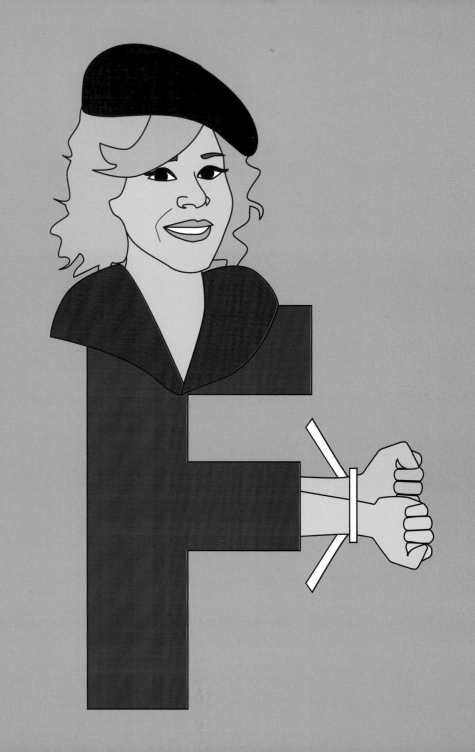

F is for Jane **F**onda. Speaking out about Native American land rights, oil drilling and global warming, this Hollywood actress, feminist and activist has continually challenged American environmental policies. Her strong commitment to eco-activism has seen her arrested many times, even in her 80s, and made her an inspiration to millions.

G is for **G**reta Thunberg. Hailed as a modern-day Joan of Arc, her 'school strike for the climate' inspired millions and made her the voice of this generation's climate change movement. The 16-year-old's confrontational speeches and inspiring leadership saw her named 'Time' magazine's Person of the Year 2019. Young legend!

H is for Julia Butterfly Hill. In 1997, she climbed a 180ft giant redwood as a one-week protest against logging. Two years later she was still there – having endured a siege, freezing rains and 40mph winds. This legendary protest saved the tree and famously inspired an episode of 'The Simpsons.'

I is for **I**ngrid Newkirk. Animal lovers stand united in appreciation for this remarkable founder of People for the Ethical Treatment of Animals (PETA). Thanks to Ingrid, cosmetic testing on animals and the use of fur have been greatly reduced, and animal welfare is now a global goal.

Jj

J is for **J**ane Goodall. Devoting 45 years to studying and protecting our closest living relatives, the 'chimpanzee lady' became a dedicated advocate of species conservation. She now uses her organization, Roots and Shoots, to encourage young people to support environmental and conservation issues.

K is for Naomi Klein. Since 2009, this influential social activist, author and filmmaker has turned her attention to environmental issues such as climate change. Her book and film, 'This Changes Everything' shone a much-needed light on the opportunity and need for economic and political transformation.

L is for **L**eonardo DiCaprio. This legendary star's eco-concerns have seen his foundation donate millions of dollars towards fighting global warming. Posting on climate-change issues almost daily on social media, Leo uses his celebrity profile to reach a wide audience and raise awareness of the urgent need for action.

M is for John Muir. America's most famous conservationist. A passionate protector of American wilderness, the 'Father of the National Parks' founded the Sierra Club, and established Yosemite and Grand Canyon National Parks so that future generations could enjoy the pristine beauty of landscapes untouched by man.

N is for Gaylord Nelson. Thanks to a genius idea by this U.S. senator in 1970, millions of people celebrate Earth Day on April 22nd every year. It's a chance for us all to unite, raise awareness of the environmental crisis facing our planet, and take action to make a difference.

O is for Ric O'Barry.
He started off his career
capturing and training
dolphins for the TV show
'Flipper.' But after one of them
died in his arms, he had an
epiphany, and has spent the
last 48 years rescuing and
rehabilitating captive dolphins
all around the world.

P is for **P**aul Watson. Always controversial, his confrontations with whaling fleets have seen him shot at, arrested and labeled an eco-terrorist. But this legendary eco-warrior still continues to use his Sea Shepherd Conservation Society to courageously protest against the cruel treatment of these beautiful creatures.

Q is for **Q**ueen of recycling, Isatou Ceesay. She taught the women of the Gambia to recycle plastic waste and turn it into beautiful wallets, purses and bags. And now, through 'Women's Initiative – The Gambia,' this inspirational legend is helping her country-women work towards achieving financial independence and greater equality.

R is for Rachel Carson. Her 1962 bestseller, 'Silent Spring,' lifted the lid on the chemical industry and raised public awareness of the harmful effects of pesticides on the environment. The resulting outcry led to a Presidential Commission and a nationwide ban on DDT for agricultural use.

S is for Irving **S**towe. Co-founding Greenpeace with his wife Dorothy, this legendary activist created the blueprint for what would become the world's largest environmental organization: a non-profit interest group with over three million members in 40 countries campaigning on issues like deforestation, nuclear weapons, whaling and climate change.

T is for **T**heodore Roosevelt. Not only was he the youngest U.S. President and inspiration behind the 'Teddy' bear, he was also a passionate conservationist. Founding the United States Forest Services and establishing 150 national forests, five national parks and 18 national monuments, he gifted America a greener future.

U is for Ursula Wolf. Passionately opposing animal testing, her paper on the 'Moral Status of Animals' defends the view that just because something may be legal and useful for humans, doesn't make it ethically correct – an argument that sits right at the heart of the animal rights movement.

V is for **V**andana Shiva. Thanks to her tireless campaigning against globalization and genetically modified crops, pesticides and herbicides, she's become a champion of the small farmers, one of 'Time' magazine's environmental heroes and the 'rock star' of the sustainable food movement. What a legend!

W is for Wangari Muta Maathai. She's the legendary eco-feminist behind the Green Belt Movement, an organization that trains women to plant trees, combat deforestation and generate income. Thanks to her vision, the movement has so far planted over 51 million trees and trained 30,000 women in forestry and other sustainable activities.

X is for **X**iuhtezcatl Martinez. 'Shoe-Tez-Caht' is a powerful voice on the front lines of the global youth-led environmental movement, Earth Guardians. He travels the world inspiring his generation to take action to save the planet, and is even suing the U.S. federal government for inaction on climate change!

Y is for Gary **Y**ourofsky. He's the animal-rights legend who converted more people to veganism than anyone else in the world. By the time he retired, he'd delivered 2,388 lectures to more than 60,000 people – but it took just one speech on animal rights in 2010 to convert 8% of Israelis to veganism!

Zz

Z is for Zoe Rosenberg. Proving age is no barrier to making a difference, this young animal-rights activist has already founded an animal sanctuary, inspired thousands of young people with her campaign for an animal bill of rights, and been named Youth Activist of the Year!

The ever-expanding legendary library

EXPLORE THESE LEGENDARY ALPHABETS & MORE AT WWW.ALPHABETLEGENDS.COM

ECO LEGENDS ALPHABET
www.alphabetlegends.com

Published by Alphabet Legends Pty Ltd in 2020
Created by Beck Feiner
Copyright © Alphabet Legends Pty Ltd 2020

UNICEF AUSTRALIA
A portion of the Net Proceeds from the sale of this book
are donated to UNICEF.

978-0-6486724-8-7

ALPHABET LEGENDS